The Power Within: A Journey to Unleashing Your Full Potential

Copyright Page

TITLE: The Power Within: A Journey to Unleashing Your Full Potential

1ST Edition

Copyright @ 2023

ISBN: 9798223425366

Table of Contents

The Power within: A journey to unleashing your full potential.

By Roberto Miguel Rodriguez

Chapter 1: Understanding Your Inner Power

Discovering the Potential Within You

Subchapter: Discovering the Potential Within You

Introduction:

In this subchapter, we will explore the incredible power that lies within each and every one of us. We are all born with innate talents, abilities, and strengths, waiting to be discovered and unleashed. By tapping into our internal potential, we can achieve extraordinary things and lead a more fulfilling life. This chapter will guide you on a journey of self-discovery, helping you unlock the power within and become everything you can be.

Unleashing Your Internal Potential:

1. Embracing Self-Awareness:

The first step in discovering your potential is to cultivate self-awareness. Take the time to reflect on your strengths, passions, and values. Understand what truly motivates and inspires you. By becoming more aware of your unique qualities, you can align your actions and decisions with your authentic self.

2. Embracing Growth Mindset:

Adopting a growth mindset is crucial for unlocking your potential. Embrace challenges, view failures as learning opportunities, and believe in your capacity to grow and improve. With a growth mindset, you can overcome obstacles and constantly push your boundaries, unleashing your true potential.

3. Identifying Your Passions:

Discovering your passions is essential for unleashing your potential. Identify activities or causes that ignite a fire within you. Whether it's art, science, entrepreneurship, or helping others, pursuing your passions will fuel your motivation and drive you towards success.

4. Setting Meaningful Goals:

Goal setting provides direction and focus in unleashing your potential. Set both short-term and long-term goals that align with your passions and values. Break them down into actionable steps and create a roadmap for achieving them. With clear goals, you can channel your potential into purposeful action.

5. Embracing Continuous Learning:

Never stop learning and growing. Seek out opportunities for personal and professional development. Read books, attend workshops, take courses, and surround yourself with individuals who inspire and challenge you. By continuously expanding your knowledge and skills, you will unlock new levels of potential within yourself.

Conclusion:

Unleashing your internal potential is a lifelong journey of self-discovery and growth. By cultivating self-awareness, embracing a growth mindset, identifying your passions, setting meaningful goals, and embracing continuous learning, you can tap into the limitless power within you. Remember, you have the ability to achieve extraordinary things and lead a truly fulfilling life. Embrace your potential, unlock your power, and become everything you can be.

Embracing Self-Awareness

In the journey of unleashing your full potential, one of the most vital tools at your disposal is self-awareness. The power to understand oneself on a deep level is the key to unlocking a world of possibilities and achieving personal growth. Self-awareness allows you to navigate through life with clarity, purpose, and authenticity. It is the foundation upon which you can build the life you truly desire.

So, what exactly is self-awareness? It is the ability to objectively observe and understand your thoughts, emotions, and behaviors. It involves being fully present in the moment, tuning into your inner voice, and gaining insights into your strengths, weaknesses, values, and beliefs. Self-awareness is not about judging or criticizing yourself; it's about cultivating a compassionate understanding of who you are and how you operate.

The journey of self-awareness begins with self-reflection. It's about taking the time to pause and explore your inner landscape. Ask yourself thought-provoking questions: What are my passions and dreams? What are my fears and limiting beliefs? What are my core values? What are the patterns and habits that hold me back? By delving into these inquiries, you will unravel layers of your being, gaining profound insights into yourself and your potential.

Self-awareness also involves accepting and embracing your true self. It's about acknowledging your strengths and weaknesses without judgment. By recognizing your strengths, you can leverage them to propel yourself forward. By acknowledging your weaknesses, you can work on them to grow and improve. Embracing your true self allows you to live authentically, aligning your actions with your values and desires.

Furthermore, self-awareness empowers you to make conscious choices. It enables you to understand the impact of your decisions on your life and those around you. By being aware of your thoughts, emotions, and behaviors, you can consciously choose to respond rather than react. This newfound awareness gives you the power to break free from old patterns and make choices that align with your goals and aspirations.

In conclusion, embracing self-awareness is a transformative journey that allows you to tap into your internal potential fully. By cultivating self-reflection, accepting your true self, and making conscious choices, you can unlock a world of possibilities and live a life of purpose and fulfillment. Embrace self-awareness, and you will embark on a powerful journey of personal growth and transformation. The power to unleash your full potential lies within you.

Recognizing Limiting Beliefs

In our journey towards realizing our full potential, one of the most critical aspects we must understand is the concept of limiting beliefs. These beliefs are the invisible barriers that hold us back from achieving greatness and reaching our true potential. They are the negative thoughts and ingrained ideas that tell us we are not capable of achieving our goals or dreams.

Recognizing and addressing these limiting beliefs is an essential step towards unleashing our internal potential. Without identifying and challenging these self-imposed limitations, we remain stuck in a cycle of self-doubt and mediocrity. However, by understanding the power of our thoughts and beliefs, we can break free from these constraints and strive towards greatness.

The first step in recognizing limiting beliefs is to become aware of our thought patterns and self-talk. Often, limiting beliefs are deeply ingrained in our subconscious mind, and we may not even be aware of their existence. By paying attention to our thoughts and the language we use when talking to ourselves, we can start identifying patterns of negative self-talk and self-limiting beliefs.

Another effective way to recognize limiting beliefs is to reflect on our past experiences and examine the patterns that emerge. Have we consistently faced similar challenges or setbacks in our lives? Do we constantly find ourselves doubting our abilities or feeling unworthy? These patterns can provide valuable insights into the underlying beliefs that are holding us back.

Once we have identified these limiting beliefs, it is crucial to challenge and reframe them. We must question the validity of these beliefs and seek evidence to counter them. For example, if we believe we are not good enough to pursue our passion, we can look for examples of people who have succeeded despite similar circumstances or limitations.

Recognizing limiting beliefs also requires us to surround ourselves with a positive and supportive environment. Negative influences and people who reinforce our self-limiting beliefs can hinder our progress. By seeking out mentors, joining supportive communities, and surrounding ourselves with like-minded individuals, we can create a positive ecosystem that encourages personal growth and challenges our limiting beliefs.

Ultimately, recognizing and overcoming limiting beliefs is a lifelong process. It requires self-awareness, introspection, and a commitment to personal growth. By understanding that these beliefs are not facts but rather self-imposed barriers, we can break free from their grasp and unleash our internal potential. It is through this recognition and transformation that we can truly become everything we are capable of being.

Cultivating a Growth Mindset

In the pursuit of personal growth and self-improvement, cultivating a growth mindset is essential. This subchapter aims to guide you on your journey to unleashing your full potential by adopting a growth mindset.

Whether you aspire to be a successful entrepreneur, a thriving artist, or simply desire to live a fulfilling life, developing a growth mindset will empower you to overcome challenges and reach new heights.

A growth mindset is the belief that our abilities and intelligence can be developed through dedication, hard work, and a willingness to learn from failures. It is the understanding that our potential is not fixed, but rather malleable, and can be expanded with effort and perseverance. Embracing a growth mindset allows us to view setbacks and obstacles as opportunities for growth, rather than as roadblocks.

To cultivate a growth mindset, it is crucial to first acknowledge and challenge any fixed beliefs or limiting thoughts that may be hindering your progress. Recognize that your abilities are not set in stone and that with the right mindset and approach, you can achieve great things. Replace thoughts of "I can't" or "I'm not good enough" with empowering affirmations such as "I am capable of learning and growing" or "I embrace challenges as opportunities for growth."

Next, surround yourself with individuals who embody a growth mindset. Seek out mentors, friends, or colleagues who inspire and motivate you to push beyond your limits. Engage in meaningful conversations, collaborate on projects, and learn from their experiences. By immersing yourself in an environment that fosters growth mindset thinking, you will be more likely to adopt these beliefs and apply them to your own life.

Furthermore, embrace failure as a stepping stone to success. Understand that setbacks and mistakes are inevitable on any journey to personal growth. Instead of dwelling on failures, view them as valuable learning experiences. Analyze what went wrong, extract the lessons, and use them to refine your approach. Remember, failure is not an indication of your worth or potential; it is merely a temporary setback that can propel you towards greater achievements.

Finally, commit to continuous learning and self-improvement. Cultivate a thirst for knowledge, seek out new experiences, and challenge yourself to step outside of your comfort zone. Embrace lifelong learning as a way to expand your horizons and unlock new opportunities. With each new skill or piece of knowledge you acquire, you will inch closer to unleashing your full potential.

In conclusion, cultivating a growth mindset is a transformative journey that empowers you to surpass your limitations and unleash your internal potential. By adopting a growth mindset, challenging fixed beliefs, surrounding yourself with growth-oriented individuals, embracing failure, and committing to continuous learning, you will pave the way for personal growth and a life filled with limitless possibilities. Embrace the power of a growth mindset, and watch as you become everything you can be.

Chapter 2: Unleashing Your Mental Strength

Harnessing the Power of Positive Thinking

In the journey towards unleashing your full potential, one of the most powerful tools at your disposal is the power of positive thinking. The way you perceive and interpret the world around you has a profound impact on your thoughts, emotions, and actions. By harnessing the power of positive thinking, you can transform your mindset, overcome challenges, and unlock your internal potential.

Positive thinking is not about denying the existence of negative experiences or pretending that everything is always perfect. Instead, it is a mindset that focuses on finding the silver lining in every situation and adopting an optimistic outlook. When faced with adversity, those who practice positive thinking are more likely to view challenges as opportunities for growth and learning.

By cultivating a positive mindset, you can rewire your brain to seek out and amplify positive experiences. This shift in perspective allows you to approach life with a greater sense of resilience, hope, and gratitude. Positive thinking empowers you to believe in your abilities, trust the process, and take proactive steps towards achieving your goals.

One of the key benefits of positive thinking is its impact on your overall well-being. Numerous studies have shown that individuals who maintain a positive mindset experience lower levels of stress, improved physical health, and increased life satisfaction. Positive thinking has also been linked to enhanced creativity, better problem-solving skills, and improved relationships with others.

To harness the power of positive thinking, it is essential to cultivate self-awareness and mindfulness. Start by paying attention to your thoughts and identifying any negative or self-limiting beliefs that may be holding you back. Challenge these beliefs by replacing them with positive affirmations and reframing negative situations as opportunities for growth.

Surround yourself with positive influences and engage in activities that bring you joy and fulfillment. Practice gratitude by reflecting on the things you are grateful for each day. Embrace a growth mindset that believes in your ability to learn, adapt, and overcome challenges.

In conclusion, harnessing the power of positive thinking is a vital component of unleashing your internal potential. By adopting an optimistic mindset, you can transform your perspective, enhance your well-being, and overcome obstacles with resilience and grace. Embrace the power of positive thinking and embark on a journey towards realizing your true capabilities.

Overcoming Self-Doubt and Fear

Introduction:

In our journey towards unleashing our full potential, one of the biggest hurdles we encounter is self-doubt and fear. These two powerful emotions can hold us back from achieving greatness and fulfilling our dreams. In this subchapter, we will explore the strategies and mindset shifts necessary to overcome self-doubt and fear, allowing us to tap into our internal potential and become everything we can be.

Understanding Self-Doubt:

Self-doubt is the voice inside our heads that tells us we are not good enough, capable enough, or deserving enough. It often stems from past experiences, societal expectations, or comparison with others.

Recognizing and acknowledging self-doubt is an essential first step towards conquering it.

Confronting Fear:

Fear, on the other hand, is an instinctual response designed to protect us from potential threats. However, it can also become a barrier that prevents us from taking risks and stepping outside our comfort zones. By understanding the difference between rational and irrational fear, we can learn to confront and conquer it.

Building Self-Confidence:

Self-confidence is the antidote to self-doubt. By focusing on our strengths, setting realistic goals, and celebrating our achievements, we can gradually build our self-confidence. Surrounding ourselves with positive and supportive people also plays a crucial role in boosting our belief in ourselves.

Changing Our Inner Dialogue:

The way we talk to ourselves has a profound impact on our self-doubt and fear. By replacing negative self-talk with positive affirmations and reframing our thoughts, we can cultivate a more empowering inner dialogue. Mindfulness and self-care practices can further help in quieting our inner critic.

Taking Action:

Taking action is the ultimate antidote to self-doubt and fear. By breaking tasks into smaller, manageable steps and taking the first step towards our goals, we build momentum and gain confidence along the way. Embracing failure as a learning opportunity and staying resilient in the face of setbacks is also crucial.

Conclusion:

Overcoming self-doubt and fear is an ongoing journey, but one that is essential for unleashing our full potential. By understanding the roots of these emotions and implementing strategies such as building self-confidence, changing our inner dialogue, and taking action, we can gradually break free from their grip. Remember, you have the power within to be everything you can be. Embrace your potential, conquer your doubts, and fearlessly pursue your dreams. The world is waiting for your greatness.

Developing Mental Resilience

In the fast-paced and ever-changing world we live in, it is crucial to develop mental resilience to navigate the challenges and uncertainties that come our way. Mental resilience allows us to bounce back from setbacks, manage stress effectively, and maintain a positive mindset, enabling us to unleash our internal potential. In this subchapter, we will explore the importance of building mental resilience and provide practical strategies to develop this essential skill.

Why is mental resilience important? Imagine a life where every setback or failure demoralizes you, leaving you feeling defeated and unable to move forward. Mental resilience empowers you to overcome adversity, learn from your experiences, and grow stronger as a result. It is the key to unlocking your full potential and becoming everything you can be.

One of the first steps in developing mental resilience is cultivating self-awareness. By understanding our thoughts, emotions, and reactions to various situations, we can identify patterns and triggers that may hinder our resilience. Self-awareness allows us to take control of our thoughts and emotions, enabling us to respond to challenges in a more constructive and resilient manner.

Another crucial aspect of mental resilience is the ability to adapt to change. The world is constantly evolving, and our ability to adapt determines our success. Embracing change and seeing it as an opportunity for growth rather than a threat can significantly enhance our mental resilience. By adopting a flexible mindset, we can navigate uncertainties with confidence and adapt our strategies accordingly.

Building a support network is equally important in developing mental resilience. Surrounding ourselves with positive and supportive individuals who believe in our potential can provide the encouragement and motivation needed during challenging times. These individuals can offer guidance, feedback, and a fresh perspective, helping us overcome obstacles and stay resilient.

Additionally, practicing self-care and stress management techniques are vital for maintaining mental resilience. Engaging in activities that bring joy and relaxation, such as exercise, meditation, or hobbies, can alleviate stress and recharge our mental batteries. Prioritizing self-care allows us to maintain a healthy balance between work, personal life, and resilience-building practices.

In conclusion, developing mental resilience is essential for unleashing your internal potential. By cultivating self-awareness, embracing change, building a support network, and prioritizing self-care, you can enhance your ability to bounce back from setbacks, manage stress effectively, and maintain a positive mindset. Remember, mental resilience is not a trait one is born with but a skill that can be developed with practice and determination. Start your journey to developing mental resilience today and unlock the power within you to become everything you can be.

Nurturing Emotional Intelligence

In the fast-paced world we live in, it is crucial to develop and nurture emotional intelligence to navigate through life successfully. Emotional intelligence, often referred to as EQ, is the ability to recognize, understand, and manage our own emotions, as well as effectively navigate relationships with others. It is an essential skill that allows us to connect with others, communicate effectively, and make wise decisions.

In "The Power Within: A Journey to Unleashing Your Full Potential," we delve into the importance of nurturing emotional intelligence to unlock your internal potential. This subchapter is dedicated to guiding you on this transformative journey towards self-discovery and personal growth.

Emotional intelligence is not something we are born with but is a skill that can be developed and honed over time. By understanding and managing our emotions, we can build stronger relationships, enhance our communication skills, and make better choices in life. This subchapter provides practical strategies and techniques to help you nurture your emotional intelligence.

Firstly, we explore self-awareness, the foundation of emotional intelligence. Through introspection and self-reflection, we delve into understanding our emotions, triggers, and patterns of behavior. By becoming more self-aware, we can better manage our emotions and respond to challenging situations with greater clarity and empathy.

Next, we delve into self-regulation, which is the ability to control and manage our emotions effectively. We provide techniques to help you develop emotional resilience, practice mindfulness, and regulate your responses to various stimuli. By mastering self-regulation, you can avoid impulsive reactions and make well-informed decisions.

Furthermore, we emphasize the importance of empathy and social awareness. Understanding the emotions and perspectives of others allows us to build stronger relationships and communicate more effectively. We provide practical tips and exercises to enhance your ability to empathize and connect with others on a deeper level.

Lastly, we explore relationship management, which involves effectively navigating and nurturing relationships. We provide insights on conflict resolution, effective communication, and building trust. By honing your relationship management skills, you can foster healthier, more fulfilling connections with those around you.

In "The Power Within: A Journey to Unleashing Your Full Potential," we believe that nurturing emotional intelligence is key to unlocking your internal potential. By developing this invaluable skill, you can enhance your personal and professional life, cultivate stronger connections, and lead a more fulfilling existence. Join us on this transformative journey towards self-discovery and embrace the power of emotional intelligence.

Chapter 3: Mastering Self-Discipline

Setting Clear Goals and Priorities

In order to unlock your full potential and become everything you can be, it is crucial to set clear goals and establish priorities. Without a roadmap to guide your journey, you may find yourself lost or aimlessly wandering through life. Setting goals and priorities provides you with a sense of purpose, direction, and clarity, allowing you to make the most of your internal potential.

Goals serve as the stepping stones towards your desired future. They give you something to strive for and help you stay focused and motivated. When setting goals, it is important to make them specific, measurable, attainable, relevant, and time-bound (SMART). By following this framework, you create a clear and actionable plan that propels you forward.

Start by envisioning what you want to achieve in different aspects of your life, such as career, relationships, health, and personal growth. Define your goals in each area and break them down into smaller, manageable tasks. This way, you can track your progress and celebrate each milestone along the way.

Prioritizing your goals is equally important. While it may be tempting to pursue multiple objectives simultaneously, spreading yourself too thin can hinder your progress. Identify the goals that align with your values and bring you closer to your ultimate vision of success. By focusing on a few key priorities at a time, you can dedicate your time, energy, and resources more effectively.

To set clear goals and establish priorities, it is crucial to reflect on your values and aspirations. What truly matters to you? What are your passions and interests? Understanding your core values and aligning them with your goals ensures that you are pursuing what truly matters to you, rather than following someone else's definition of success.

Additionally, it is important to regularly review and adjust your goals and priorities. As you evolve and grow, your aspirations may change. Be open to reassessing your objectives and adapting them to your current circumstances. This flexibility allows you to stay on track and make the necessary adjustments to ensure you are consistently moving towards unleashing your full potential.

In conclusion, setting clear goals and establishing priorities are essential steps on your journey to unleashing your internal potential. They provide you with direction, focus, and motivation. By defining your goals, prioritizing them, and aligning them with your values, you can unlock the power within and become everything you can be. Remember, the journey towards your full potential starts with a clear vision and a plan to turn that vision into reality.

Creating Effective Habits

In order to unleash your internal potential and become everything you can be, it is crucial to develop effective habits that support your growth and success. Habits are powerful forces that shape our lives, determine our outcomes, and define who we are as individuals. By understanding how habits work and implementing strategies to create effective ones, you can transform your life and tap into the power within.

The first step in creating effective habits is to identify your goals and aspirations. What do you want to achieve in your personal and professional life? Once you have a clear vision of your desired outcomes, you can align your habits with those goals. For example, if you aspire to become a successful entrepreneur, you can develop a habit of reading books on business and networking with like-minded individuals.

Another key aspect of creating effective habits is to start small and build momentum. Often, people make the mistake of trying to overhaul their entire life overnight, which can lead to overwhelm and ultimately failure. Instead, focus on developing one habit at a time. Start with something simple, such as waking up 30 minutes earlier each day to engage in a morning routine that promotes productivity and mindfulness. Once this habit becomes ingrained, you can move on to the next one.

Consistency is the key to making habits stick. It takes time and effort to create lasting change, so it is important to commit to your new habits every day. Set reminders, create accountability systems, and find ways to stay motivated. Surround yourself with people who support your journey and share similar goals. By integrating your new habits into your daily routine, they will become second nature, and you will reap the rewards of your efforts.

Lastly, be kind to yourself throughout this process. Habits take time to form, and setbacks are a natural part of the journey. Instead of beating yourself up over a missed day or a slip-up, focus on getting back on track and staying committed to your goals. Remember that every small step counts, and each day is an opportunity to create positive change.

By creating effective habits, you will unleash your internal potential and become everything you can be. Your habits will shape your character, determine your success, and lead you towards a life of fulfillment and purpose. Embrace the power within you and start building the habits that will transform your life.

Managing Time Efficiently

In today's fast-paced world, time is an invaluable resource that often seems to slip through our fingers. We find ourselves overwhelmed by endless to-do lists and deadlines, struggling to balance our personal and professional lives. However, by learning to manage our time efficiently, we can unlock our full potential and become everything we aspire to be.

This subchapter explores the art of time management, providing practical strategies and techniques that can help anyone gain control over their schedule and make the most of each precious moment. Whether you are a student, a professional, a stay-at-home parent, or an aspiring entrepreneur, this chapter is designed to equip you with the tools you need to maximize your productivity and achieve your goals.

The journey to managing time efficiently begins with self-awareness. By understanding our priorities, strengths, and weaknesses, we can identify areas where our time is being wasted or misused. This subchapter delves into self-reflection exercises and prompts that encourage readers to evaluate their current time management habits and make necessary adjustments.

Next, we delve into proven time management techniques such as the Pomodoro Technique, Eisenhower Matrix, and setting SMART goals. These methods empower individuals to break tasks into manageable chunks, prioritize effectively, and eliminate time-wasting activities. We also explore the power of delegation and outsourcing, teaching readers how to leverage their strengths by leveraging the skills and talents of others.

Moreover, this subchapter emphasizes the importance of setting boundaries and learning to say no. By understanding our limitations and not overcommitting, we can create a schedule that allows us to focus on what truly matters. Time-blocking and creating a daily routine are also addressed, providing readers with practical strategies to structure their days for maximum productivity.

Furthermore, the subchapter delves into the role of technology in time management. We discuss the benefits and drawbacks of various digital tools and apps that can streamline tasks, automate processes, and help us stay organized. From calendar apps to project management software, readers will gain insights into how technology can be harnessed to enhance their time management skills.

In conclusion, managing time efficiently is a crucial skill that can unlock our full potential. This subchapter equips readers with the necessary knowledge and techniques to take control of their schedules, eliminate procrastination, and achieve their goals. By implementing the strategies outlined in this chapter, readers will be empowered to become everything they can be – unleashing their internal potential and living a more fulfilling, purpose-driven life.

Staying Committed to Personal Growth

In the fast-paced world we live in today, it's easy to get caught up in the daily grind and lose sight of our personal growth. However, if we truly want to unleash our internal potential and be everything we can be, it is essential to stay committed to our personal growth journey. This subchapter aims to provide valuable insights and practical tips to help you stay committed to your personal growth, no matter what challenges come your way.

One of the first steps to staying committed to personal growth is to set clear goals. By clearly defining what you want to achieve and the steps you need to take to get there, you create a roadmap for your personal growth journey. These goals should be specific, measurable, attainable, relevant, and time-bound (SMART goals), allowing you to track your progress and stay motivated.

Another key aspect of staying committed to personal growth is cultivating a growth mindset. Embracing the belief that you can continuously learn, improve, and develop new skills will help you overcome obstacles and setbacks along the way. By viewing challenges as opportunities for growth rather than failures, you'll maintain a positive attitude and remain dedicated to your personal growth journey.

Consistency is crucial when it comes to personal growth. It's not enough to make sporadic efforts; instead, you need to establish daily habits that support your growth. This could include reading books or articles related to your interests, attending workshops or seminars, or dedicating time each day to reflect and set new goals. By incorporating these habits into your routine, personal growth becomes a natural part of your life.

Surrounding yourself with like-minded individuals who support your personal growth is also essential. Seek out mentors or join communities that share your goals and values. These connections will provide encouragement, guidance, and accountability, ensuring you stay committed to your path of personal growth.

Finally, it's important to celebrate your progress along the way. Acknowledge the small victories and milestones you achieve, as this will boost your motivation and remind you of the progress you've made. Personal growth is a lifelong journey, so take the time to appreciate how far you've come while staying focused on the road ahead.

In conclusion, staying committed to personal growth is vital for unleashing your internal potential and becoming everything you can be. By setting clear goals, cultivating a growth mindset, maintaining consistency, surrounding yourself with supportive individuals, and celebrating your progress, you'll ensure that personal growth remains a constant part of your life. Embrace this journey wholeheartedly, and watch as you unleash your true power within.

Chapter 4: Embracing Change and Adaptability

Embracing the Beauty of Impermanence

In our fast-paced, ever-changing world, we often find ourselves yearning for stability and permanence. We strive to hold onto the people, things, and situations that bring comfort and familiarity to our lives. However, what if we were to shift our perspective and embrace the beauty of impermanence?

This subchapter explores the profound concept of embracing impermanence as a means of unlocking our full potential. It challenges the notion that permanence is essential for happiness and fulfillment, and instead encourages us to find beauty and strength in the transient nature of life.

Within the pages of "The Power Within: A Journey to Unleashing Your Full Potential," readers are invited to explore the profound impact that embracing impermanence can have on their personal growth and self-discovery. The author delves into the idea that by recognizing and accepting the impermanence of all things, we can cultivate a mindset that is open, adaptable, and resilient.

The book addresses the public audience, particularly those seeking personal development and self-improvement within the niche of "BE EVERYTHING YOU CAN BE: UNLEASHING YOUR INTERNAL POTENTIAL." It aims to empower readers to embrace change and uncertainty, rather than fearing them. By doing so, they can tap into their internal potential and discover new opportunities for growth and transformation.

Through insightful anecdotes, practical exercises, and thought-provoking questions, the author guides readers on a transformative journey. They learn to let go of attachment to outcomes, to appreciate the present moment, and to find joy in the ever-changing nature of life.

By embracing impermanence, readers are encouraged to explore new possibilities, take risks, and step out of their comfort zones. They discover that impermanence is not something to be feared but rather a powerful force that propels them towards personal and professional growth.

"The Power Within: A Journey to Unleashing Your Full Potential" serves as a guiding light for those seeking to navigate the complexities of life with grace and resilience. It reminds us that within the impermanence lies the beauty of endless possibilities, growth, and transformation.

In this subchapter, readers will find the inspiration and guidance they need to embrace impermanence fully. By doing so, they can unleash their internal potential and create a life that is vibrant, fulfilling, and abundant.

Letting Go of the Need for Control

In our relentless pursuit of success and fulfillment, we often find ourselves caught in the grip of an overwhelming desire for control. We strive to control our circumstances, our relationships, and even ourselves, believing that this will bring us the happiness and satisfaction we seek. However, what if I told you that the key to unlocking your true potential lies in letting go of this need for control?

In this subchapter, we will explore the profound impact that relinquishing control can have on our journey towards unleashing our internal potential. It is a concept that may seem counterintuitive at first, but it is one that holds immense power and liberation.

When we cling tightly to the need for control, we limit our ability to adapt and grow. We become trapped in a rigid mindset that stifles creativity and innovation, preventing us from exploring new possibilities and reaching our full potential. By releasing our grip on control, we open ourselves up to a world of infinite opportunities and experiences.

Letting go of the need for control also frees us from the burden of expectations. We often place unrealistic expectations on ourselves and others, leading to disappointment and frustration. By embracing a more flexible and open mindset, we can accept the uncertainties of life and find peace in the present moment.

It is important to recognize that letting go of control does not mean surrendering to chaos or abandoning responsibility. It means relinquishing our attachment to outcomes and embracing the journey itself. We learn to trust in our own abilities and in the universe, allowing things to unfold naturally while remaining proactive and intentional in our actions.

In this subchapter, we will explore practical strategies for letting go of control, such as cultivating mindfulness, practicing acceptance, and embracing vulnerability. We will also delve into the psychological and emotional benefits of releasing the need for control, including increased resilience, improved relationships, and a greater sense of fulfillment.

So, if you are ready to break free from the shackles of control and tap into your true potential, join us on this transformative journey of letting go. Together, we will discover the power that lies within us when we surrender and allow life's beautiful mysteries to unfold. Get ready to unleash your full potential and become everything you can be.

Adapting to Unexpected Situations

Life is full of surprises, some of which can catch us off guard and leave us feeling overwhelmed or uncertain. However, it is during these moments of unexpected situations that our true potential shines through. In this subchapter, we will explore the importance of adapting to unexpected situations and how it can help us unleash our full potential.

Life has a funny way of throwing curveballs at us when we least expect it. Whether it's a sudden change in career, a personal loss, or a global pandemic, these unexpected situations can challenge us to the core. But instead of succumbing to fear or despair, we have the power to adapt and overcome.

Adapting to unexpected situations requires a shift in mindset. It is about embracing change and viewing it as an opportunity for growth rather than a setback. When we open ourselves up to new possibilities, we tap into our internal potential and discover strengths we never knew we had.

The key to adapting is to remain flexible. Just as a tree bends with the wind, we must be willing to adjust our plans and expectations when circumstances change. This may involve letting go of our attachment to a specific outcome and embracing the uncertainty of the unknown. By doing so, we create space for creativity and innovation to thrive.

In times of unexpected situations, it is crucial to stay resilient. Resilience is the ability to bounce back from setbacks and adversity. It enables us to face challenges head-on, learn from our mistakes, and keep moving forward. Resilience is not about avoiding failure but rather embracing it as a stepping stone towards success.

Furthermore, adapting to unexpected situations often requires us to step outside of our comfort zones. It pushes us to explore new avenues, develop new skills, and expand our horizons. By challenging ourselves and embracing the unknown, we unlock our hidden potential and discover what we are truly capable of achieving.

In conclusion, adapting to unexpected situations is a fundamental aspect of unleashing our internal potential. It requires us to shift our mindset, remain flexible, stay resilient, and embrace the unknown. When we approach unexpected situations with an open mind and an unwavering spirit, we not only survive but thrive. So, let us embrace life's surprises and unlock the power within us to be everything we can be.

Thriving in a Changing World

In the fast-paced, ever-evolving world we live in, it is essential to not just survive but thrive. The ability to adapt and embrace change is crucial for individuals seeking to unleash their internal potential and be everything they can be. In this subchapter, "Thriving in a Changing World," we will explore the mindset and skills needed to navigate the challenges and opportunities that arise in an ever-shifting landscape.

Change can often be intimidating and overwhelming, but it is important to remember that it is an inevitable part of life. Rather than resisting or fearing it, we must learn to embrace change as an opportunity for growth and self-improvement. By developing a mindset that is open to new experiences and possibilities, we can unlock our full potential and thrive in any situation.

One of the key skills required to thrive in a changing world is adaptability. This involves being flexible and willing to adjust our plans and strategies when circumstances demand it. By being adaptable, we can easily pivot and find innovative solutions to challenges that arise. It is about being proactive rather than reactive, and constantly seeking to improve and learn from our experiences.

Another vital skill for thriving in a changing world is resilience. Change often brings uncertainty and setbacks, but it is our ability to bounce back and persevere that separates those who merely survive from those who thrive. Cultivating resilience involves developing a positive mindset, practicing self-care, and building a support system that encourages growth and development.

Additionally, thriving in a changing world requires a commitment to continuous learning and self-improvement. The world is constantly evolving, and to stay ahead, we must be willing to acquire new knowledge, learn new skills, and adapt to emerging trends. This could involve attending workshops, reading books, taking online courses, or seeking mentorship from experts in our chosen field.

Ultimately, thriving in a changing world is not just about surviving but embracing the opportunities that change brings. It is about unleashing our internal potential and becoming everything we can be. By adopting an adaptable mindset, cultivating resilience, and committing to continuous learning, we can navigate the ever-changing landscape and thrive in our personal and professional lives.

So, dear readers, I invite you to embrace the challenges and opportunities that come your way, and embark on a journey of self-discovery and growth. The power to thrive in a changing world lies within you. Unleash it, and be everything you can be.

Chapter 5: Cultivating a Positive Mindset

Practicing Gratitude and Appreciation

In our pursuit to unleash our full potential, it is important to recognize the power of gratitude and appreciation in our lives. These simple yet profound practices have the ability to transform our mindset, uplift our spirits, and bring about positive changes in every aspect of our existence. In this subchapter, we will explore the significance of practicing gratitude and appreciation, and how it can help us become everything we can be.

Gratitude is the act of acknowledging and being thankful for the blessings, opportunities, and even the challenges that life presents us with. It is about shifting our focus from what we lack to what we have, cultivating a sense of abundance and contentment. By practicing gratitude, we train our minds to look for the good in every situation, fostering a positive attitude and attracting more positivity into our lives.

Appreciation, on the other hand, is the act of recognizing and valuing the people, experiences, and things that bring us joy and fulfillment. It involves expressing our gratitude towards others and acknowledging their contributions to our lives. When we appreciate the efforts and kindness of those around us, we foster stronger relationships, create a sense of belonging, and inspire others to continue spreading positivity.

Both gratitude and appreciation are powerful tools for personal growth and development. They not only enhance our mental and emotional well-being but also have a profound impact on our physical health. Studies have shown that practicing gratitude and appreciation can reduce stress levels, improve sleep quality, boost immune function, and increase overall happiness.

In this subchapter, we will delve into various techniques and exercises that can help us incorporate gratitude and appreciation into our daily lives. From keeping a gratitude journal to practicing random acts of kindness, we will explore practical strategies that can make these practices a natural part of our existence.

By embracing the power of gratitude and appreciation, we can unlock our internal potential and cultivate a mindset of abundance and fulfillment. Our relationships will flourish, our resilience will strengthen, and our overall well-being will skyrocket. Let us embark on this journey of practicing gratitude and appreciation, and witness the transformative power it has in unleashing our true potential.

Remember, gratitude is not just a one-time act; it is a way of life. So, let us begin this beautiful journey together, and watch as our lives become a testament to the incredible power within us.

Developing a Resilient Attitude

In our journey to unleash our internal potential and become everything we can be, one trait that is absolutely essential is resilience. Life is full of challenges, setbacks, and obstacles that can easily discourage us, but with a resilient attitude, we can overcome any adversity that comes our way.

Resilience is the ability to bounce back from difficult situations, to adapt and grow in the face of adversity. It is not a trait that some people are born with and others are not; rather, it is a skill that can be cultivated and developed over time. In this subchapter, we will explore various strategies and techniques to help you develop a resilient attitude and navigate through the ups and downs of life.

First and foremost, it is important to understand that setbacks are a natural part of life. Instead of dwelling on them or viewing them as failures, we must reframe our mindset and see them as opportunities for growth and learning. By changing our perspective, we can transform setbacks into stepping stones towards success.

Another crucial aspect of developing resilience is building a strong support network. Surrounding yourself with positive, like-minded individuals who believe in your potential can provide you with the encouragement and motivation needed to persevere. Sharing your struggles and triumphs with others not only helps you gain valuable insights but also reminds you that you are not alone in your journey.

Additionally, self-care plays a vital role in developing resilience. Taking care of your physical, mental, and emotional well-being is essential for building the strength necessary to face challenges head-on. Engaging in activities that bring you joy, practicing mindfulness and meditation, and prioritizing self-reflection and self-improvement are all powerful ways to nurture your resilience.

Lastly, reframing failure as feedback is a crucial mindset shift in developing a resilient attitude. Instead of seeing failure as a reflection of your worth, view it as an opportunity to learn, grow, and improve. Embrace the lessons that failure offers and use them to fuel your determination and drive.

In conclusion, developing a resilient attitude is essential in our journey to unleash our internal potential. By reframing setbacks, building a support network, prioritizing self-care, and embracing failure as feedback, we can cultivate the strength and resilience needed to overcome any obstacle that comes our way. Remember, resilience is not about avoiding challenges, but rather about facing them head-on and emerging stronger and more empowered than ever before.

Fostering Optimism and Hope

In our journey to unleashing our full potential, one crucial aspect that we often overlook is the power of optimism and hope. These two qualities have the ability to transform our lives and enable us to become everything we can be. In this subchapter, we will explore the significance of fostering optimism and hope and how they can propel us towards our desired goals.

Optimism, the belief that things will work out for the best, is a mindset that can open doors to endless possibilities. By cultivating a positive outlook on life, we can overcome obstacles, stay motivated, and maintain a sense of resilience even in the face of adversity. Optimism allows us to view setbacks as opportunities for growth, and failure as a stepping stone to success. By embracing optimism, we can tap into our internal potential and unlock a world of possibilities that we never thought possible.

Hope, on the other hand, acts as the fuel that keeps our dreams alive. It is the unwavering belief that our goals and aspirations can be accomplished. Without hope, our journey towards self-actualization becomes dull and uninspiring. Hope instills in us the courage to take risks, to step out of our comfort zone, and to persist even when the road ahead seems uncertain. It empowers us to keep moving forward, knowing that every step we take brings us one step closer to realizing our true potential.

To foster optimism and hope, it is essential to surround ourselves with positive influences. Seek out individuals who radiate positivity and inspire you to be the best version of yourself. Engage in activities that bring you joy and fulfillment, as they will naturally cultivate a positive mindset. Practice gratitude and mindfulness, as these practices can shift our focus towards the present moment and help us appreciate the blessings in our lives.

Remember that fostering optimism and hope is a continuous process. It requires effort and commitment to maintain a positive outlook, especially during challenging times. But by doing so, we create a ripple effect that not only transforms our own lives but also impacts those around us. By embracing optimism and hope, we become beacons of light in a world that often feels dark and uncertain.

So, let us embark on this journey of fostering optimism and hope, knowing that by doing so, we are unlocking our true potential and becoming everything we can be. Together, let us radiate positivity, inspire others, and create a brighter, more hopeful world.

Finding Silver Linings in Challenges

Life is full of ups and downs, and it's during the challenging times that we often find ourselves questioning our abilities and potential. However, it is precisely during these moments of adversity that we have the opportunity to discover our true strengths and unleash our internal potential. In this subchapter, we will explore the concept of finding silver linings in challenges and how it can empower us to become everything we can be.

Challenges are not meant to break us; they are meant to shape us. They push us out of our comfort zones and force us to confront our fears and limitations. It is in these moments that we have the chance to redefine ourselves and tap into our hidden potential. When faced with a difficult situation, rather than dwelling on the negative, we can train ourselves to focus on the positive aspects or silver linings.

Finding silver linings in challenges requires a shift in perspective. Instead of seeing obstacles as roadblocks, we can view them as opportunities for growth and self-improvement. For example, a setback in our career can be seen as a chance to explore new paths and discover hidden talents. A personal loss can lead us to cherish our loved ones and appreciate the preciousness of life. By reframing our mindset, we can transform challenges into stepping stones towards our full potential.

Moreover, challenges teach us valuable life lessons. They provide us with the tools and experiences necessary to navigate future obstacles. When faced with adversity, it's important to reflect on the lessons learned and apply them to future situations. Each challenge we overcome strengthens our resilience and equips us with the wisdom needed to face future obstacles with confidence.

To fully unleash our internal potential, we must embrace challenges as opportunities for growth. It is through these experiences that we discover our true capabilities and learn to harness the power within us. By finding silver linings in challenges, we can develop a positive mindset, cultivate resilience, and become everything we can be.

In conclusion, challenges are not to be feared, but to be embraced. They hold the key to unlocking our full potential and unleashing the power within us. By shifting our perspective and finding silver linings in challenges, we can transform adversity into opportunities for growth and self-discovery. So, the next time you face a challenge, remember to look for the silver lining and use it as a stepping stone towards becoming everything you can be.

Chapter 6: Building Confidence and Self-Esteem

Recognizing and Overcoming Self-Limiting Beliefs

In our journey towards unleashing our internal potential, one of the most significant obstacles we encounter is our own self-limiting beliefs. These beliefs, often ingrained in our minds from a young age, can hinder our growth and prevent us from reaching our full potential. However, by recognizing and addressing these self-imposed limitations, we can break free from their constraints and unlock the power within us.

Self-limiting beliefs are the negative thoughts and assumptions we hold about ourselves, our abilities, and what we can achieve. They stem from past experiences, societal conditioning, and fear of failure. These beliefs can manifest in various ways, such as thinking we are not smart enough, not talented enough, or not deserving of success. They create a mental barrier that keeps us trapped in a cycle of self-doubt and prevents us from taking risks or pursuing our dreams.

The first step to overcoming self-limiting beliefs is to become aware of them. Take a moment to reflect on your thoughts and identify any negative patterns or beliefs that are holding you back. Once you have recognized these limiting beliefs, challenge them. Ask yourself if there is any evidence to support these beliefs or if they are simply assumptions rooted in fear.

Next, replace these self-limiting beliefs with empowering ones. Affirmations and positive self-talk can be powerful tools in this process. Repeat statements that reinforce your potential, such as "I am capable of achieving great things" or "I deserve success." By consistently reinforcing these positive beliefs, you can rewire your subconscious mind and overcome the self-imposed limitations that have been holding you back.

Additionally, surround yourself with a supportive network of individuals who believe in your potential. Seek out mentors, coaches, or like-minded individuals who can offer guidance and encouragement. Their belief in you can help challenge your self-limiting beliefs and inspire you to reach higher.

Remember, overcoming self-limiting beliefs is an ongoing process. As you push your boundaries and achieve new successes, new beliefs may arise. Stay vigilant and continue to challenge and replace these limiting beliefs to unleash your full potential.

In conclusion, recognizing and overcoming self-limiting beliefs is crucial to unleashing our internal potential. By becoming aware of these beliefs, challenging them, and replacing them with empowering thoughts, we can break free from the constraints that hold us back. With the support of a positive network, we can continue to grow and achieve greatness. Embrace the power within you, and step into the limitless possibilities that await on your journey to becoming everything you can be.

Embracing Self-Acceptance and Self-Love

In a world that often emphasizes external achievements and societal expectations, it is easy to lose sight of our true worth and potential. The subchapter "Embracing Self-Acceptance and Self-Love" from the book "The Power Within: A Journey to Unleashing Your Full Potential" is a guiding light for those seeking to unleash their internal potential and be everything they can be.

At its core, self-acceptance is about recognizing and embracing who we truly are, with all our strengths, weaknesses, and imperfections. It is a fundamental step towards personal growth and unleashing our full potential. By accepting ourselves, we free ourselves from the burden of comparison, judgment, and the need for external validation. We acknowledge that we are unique individuals on our own unique paths, and that is something to be celebrated.

Self-love plays a vital role in this journey as well. It involves practicing compassion, kindness, and forgiveness towards ourselves. It means treating ourselves with the same care and respect we would give to others. By cultivating self-love, we create a strong foundation for personal growth, as it allows us to nurture our desires, dreams, and aspirations. It empowers us to set healthy boundaries, make choices aligned with our values, and pursue what truly brings us joy and fulfillment.

This subchapter explores various practical strategies and exercises to cultivate self-acceptance and self-love. It encourages readers to embark on a journey of self-discovery, exploring their passions, interests, and values. It emphasizes the importance of embracing vulnerability and learning from failures, as they are stepping stones towards growth. It also provides guidance on practicing self-care, setting boundaries, and developing a positive self-image.

Addressing the public and the niches of "BE EVERYTHING YOU CAN BE: UNLEASHING YOUR INTERNAL POTENTIAL," this subchapter resonates with individuals who are seeking personal growth, fulfillment, and a deeper understanding of themselves. It serves as a reminder that our worth is not dependent on external achievements or societal standards. Rather, it lies within us, waiting to be discovered and embraced.

By embracing self-acceptance and self-love, readers are empowered to unleash their internal potential. They are encouraged to step into their authentic selves, embrace their unique qualities, and pursue a life that aligns with their true desires. In doing so, they embark on a transformative journey towards unlocking their full potential and becoming everything they can be.

Celebrating Personal Achievements

Subchapter: Celebrating Personal Achievements

Introduction:

In our journey towards unleashing our full potential, it is crucial to acknowledge and celebrate our personal achievements. Celebrating these milestones not only boosts our confidence but also serves as a reminder of our progress and the power that lies within us. In this subchapter, we will explore the importance of celebrating personal achievements and how it can contribute to our journey of becoming everything we can be.

Recognizing Your Accomplishments:

Each one of us has unique talents, dreams, and aspirations. No matter how big or small, every achievement deserves recognition. By acknowledging our accomplishments, we affirm our abilities and the steps we have taken to reach our goals. Whether it is completing a challenging project, overcoming a personal fear, or achieving a significant milestone, celebrating these achievements strengthens our belief in ourselves and fuels our motivation to continue striving for greatness.

The Power of Gratitude:

Celebrating personal achievements goes beyond mere self-congratulation. It is an opportunity to express gratitude towards ourselves and those who have supported us throughout our journey. Gratitude not only cultivates a positive mindset but also enhances our overall well-being. By recognizing and appreciating the efforts we have invested in our personal growth, we gain a deeper sense of fulfillment and joy.

Inspiring Others:

As we celebrate our personal achievements, we have the power to inspire others. Our successes can serve as a testament to the possibilities that lie within each individual. By openly sharing our accomplishments and the challenges we have overcome, we ignite a spark in others, encouraging them to embark on their own journeys towards self-discovery and personal growth. Through our celebrations, we create a ripple effect, inspiring a community to unleash their internal potential.

Creating Milestones for Future Growth:

Celebrating personal achievements is not only a reflection of past successes but also a stepping stone for future growth. By acknowledging our accomplishments, we gain clarity on our capabilities and areas of improvement. This introspection allows us to set new goals, push our boundaries, and continue evolving into the best version of ourselves.

Conclusion:

In the pursuit of unleashing our internal potential, celebrating personal achievements is an essential component. It empowers us to recognize our progress, fosters gratitude, inspires others, and acts as a catalyst for continued growth. Let us embrace the power within us by celebrating our achievements and encouraging others to do the same. Together, we can create a world where everyone strives to become everything they can be.

Surrounding Yourself with Supportive Relationships

In the pursuit of unleashing your internal potential, one crucial aspect that often goes overlooked is the influence of our relationships. The people we surround ourselves with play a significant role in shaping our mindset, beliefs, and ultimately our success. Whether it is personal or professional, having a support system that encourages and uplifts us is essential for unlocking our full potential.

When it comes to personal relationships, we need individuals who believe in us unconditionally. These are the people who see our worth and potential, even when we struggle to recognize it ourselves. Surrounding ourselves with such individuals can boost our self-confidence and provide the necessary motivation to overcome obstacles. They offer a shoulder to lean on during challenging times and celebrate our successes, no matter how small. These relationships act as a safety net, providing emotional support and helping us maintain a positive outlook on life.

Furthermore, supportive relationships extend beyond our personal lives into our professional endeavors. In the workplace, having colleagues or mentors who believe in our capabilities can significantly impact our performance and growth. They can offer guidance, share valuable insights, and provide opportunities for advancement. By surrounding ourselves with ambitious and driven individuals, we are more likely to adopt their mindset and push ourselves further. Such relationships can open doors to new possibilities, expand our network, and expose us to different perspectives.

However, it is crucial to remember that supportive relationships are not one-sided. It is equally important to reciprocate the support and encouragement we receive. By actively nurturing these relationships, we create a mutually beneficial environment where everyone can thrive. This involves offering a listening ear, providing constructive feedback, and celebrating the achievements of those around us. When we give support, we receive it in return, creating a reinforcing cycle of growth and empowerment.

To cultivate supportive relationships, it is essential to be proactive. Seek out individuals who inspire you, share similar goals, and genuinely care about your success. Attend networking events, join professional organizations, or engage in activities aligned with your interests. Actively invest time and effort in building and maintaining these relationships, as they are vital for unleashing your internal potential.

In conclusion, surrounding yourself with supportive relationships is a fundamental aspect of unleashing your internal potential. Whether personally or professionally, these relationships provide the necessary encouragement, motivation, and guidance to overcome obstacles and achieve success. By reciprocating the support we receive and actively investing in these relationships, we create a supportive network that fosters growth and unleashes our full potential. Remember, it is through the power of these relationships that we can truly be everything we aspire to be.

Chapter 7: Tapping into Your Passion and Purpose

Identifying Your Passions and Interests

In our fast-paced and ever-changing world, it can be easy to lose sight of our true passions and interests. We often find ourselves caught up in the daily grind, going through the motions without truly experiencing the joy and fulfillment that comes from pursuing what truly excites us. But deep within each of us lies a wellspring of untapped potential, waiting to be unleashed. It is time to embark on a journey of self-discovery and identify the passions and interests that will lead us to unleash our full potential.

Discovering what truly excites us is the first step towards living a life of purpose and fulfillment. It is about becoming aware of the activities that make us lose track of time, the topics that ignite our curiosity, and the causes that ignite our passion. These are the clues that will guide us towards our true passions and interests.

To begin this journey, we must take the time for self-reflection and introspection. What activities do we find ourselves naturally gravitating towards? What topics do we find ourselves diving into with enthusiasm? What things do we enjoy doing in our leisure time? By exploring our own innate inclinations, we can gain valuable insights into what truly excites us.

Additionally, seeking new experiences and stepping out of our comfort zones can also help us uncover hidden passions and interests. Trying out new hobbies, exploring different cultures, and engaging in diverse activities can open our minds to new possibilities and spark new passions within us.

Moreover, it is essential to pay attention to the emotions and feelings that arise when we engage in certain activities or pursue specific interests. Do we feel a sense of joy, fulfillment, and purpose? Do we feel a sense of flow and timelessness? These positive emotions are indicators that we are on the right track towards identifying our passions and interests.

Lastly, it is crucial to remember that identifying our passions and interests is a continuous process. As we grow and evolve, our interests may change, and new passions may emerge. Therefore, we must remain open-minded and adaptable, always willing to explore new avenues and embrace new passions.

Identifying our passions and interests is the key to unleashing our internal potential. When we align our lives with what truly excites us, we tap into a wellspring of energy, creativity, and motivation. We become unstoppable, driven by a sense of purpose and fulfillment that propels us towards our dreams. So, let us embark on this journey of self-discovery, uncover our passions and interests, and unleash our full potential. The power to live a life of fulfillment and success lies within us.

Discovering Your Life's Purpose

Subchapter: Discovering Your Life's Purpose

Introduction:

Welcome to the subchapter on discovering your life's purpose, where we will explore the profound journey of uncovering your true calling and unleashing your internal potential. In this chapter, we will delve deep into the essential questions that can guide you towards a life of fulfillment and meaning. Whether you are a student, a working professional, or someone seeking a fresh start, this subchapter is designed to help you connect with your innermost desires and find your unique purpose in life.

Understanding the Importance of Purpose:

Life without purpose can feel like drifting aimlessly in a vast ocean. However, when you discover your life's purpose, everything changes. Purpose provides a sense of direction, motivation, and fulfillment, allowing you to live a life aligned with your truest self. It is the driving force behind your actions, the source of inspiration that propels you forward even in the face of challenges.

Exploring Your Passions and Talents:

To discover your life's purpose, it's essential to explore your passions and talents. What activities make you lose track of time? What brings you joy and fulfillment? Reflect on your past experiences, hobbies, and interests that have consistently energized you. Identifying your passions and talents will help you uncover potential avenues that align with your purpose.

Defining Your Values and Beliefs:

Understanding your core values and beliefs is another crucial aspect of discovering your life's purpose. Your values define what is most important to you, while your beliefs shape your perspective on life. Take time to reflect on what truly matters to you, and explore how you can align your purpose with your values and beliefs. This alignment will provide a solid foundation for a purpose-driven life.

Listening to Your Intuition:

Intuition is a powerful guiding force that can lead you towards your life's purpose. It is that inner voice, that gut feeling, which often knows what you truly desire. Cultivating mindfulness and practicing self-reflection can help you tap into your intuition. Pay attention to the whispers of your heart and follow the path that feels right for you.

Taking Action:

Discovering your life's purpose is not just about introspection; it also requires taking action. Start by setting small, achievable goals that align with your purpose. Each step you take will bring you closer to your true calling. Embrace the journey and be open to new experiences and opportunities along the way.

Conclusion:

Finding your life's purpose is a transformative process that can unlock your full potential. It requires self-reflection, exploration, and a willingness to listen to your inner voice. Remember, your purpose may evolve over time, but the key is to embark on the journey and embrace the limitless possibilities that await you. Discovering your life's purpose will not only bring you personal fulfillment but also enable you to contribute positively to the world around you. So, let us embark on this journey together and unleash the power within to become everything you can be.

Aligning Your Actions with Your Values

In our journey towards unleashing our full potential, one crucial aspect that often gets overlooked is aligning our actions with our values. Our values act as the compass that guides us towards living a truly fulfilling and purposeful life. When we align our actions with these values, we unlock a powerful force within us that propels us towards success, fulfillment, and inner peace.

But what exactly does it mean to align our actions with our values? It means living in congruence with what we believe in, making choices and decisions that are in line with our core principles. It's about ensuring that our daily actions reflect the things that truly matter to us.

Aligning our actions with our values requires self-reflection and introspection. It starts with identifying our core values - those principles that define who we are and what we stand for. These values could be honesty, integrity, compassion, growth, or any other guiding principles that resonate with us at a deep level. Once we have identified our values, we can then evaluate our actions and behaviors to see if they align with these values.

When our actions are not in alignment with our values, we often experience a sense of discontentment and inner conflict. We may find ourselves feeling unfulfilled, even if we achieve external success. This misalignment can lead to a lack of purpose and a constant feeling of being off-track. On the other hand, when our actions are in harmony with our values, we experience a sense of fulfillment, authenticity, and joy.

To align our actions with our values, we must be willing to make conscious choices and decisions. This may involve stepping out of our comfort zones, letting go of unhealthy habits, or reevaluating our priorities. It requires us to be honest with ourselves and take responsibility for the choices we make.

Remember, aligning our actions with our values is an ongoing process. It requires regular self-reflection, as our values may evolve and change over time. It also requires us to be mindful of our actions and constantly evaluate whether they are in alignment with our values.

When we align our actions with our values, we tap into a powerful source of motivation and inspiration. We become more focused, resilient, and driven towards our goals. By living in congruence with our values, we unleash our internal potential and become everything we can be.

In conclusion, aligning your actions with your values is an essential step towards unleashing your full potential. It requires self-reflection, conscious choices, and a commitment to living in congruence with your core principles. When you align your actions with your values, you unlock a powerful force within you that propels you towards success, fulfillment, and inner peace. So, take the time to identify your values and evaluate your actions - and watch as you become everything you can be.

Igniting the Fire Within

In our fast-paced world, it is easy to get caught up in the daily grind and forget about the immense potential that lies within each and every one of us. We often find ourselves living on autopilot, going through the motions without truly tapping into our internal power. However, it is crucial to understand that within us lies a fire, a burning desire to become everything we can be.

Welcome to the subchapter, "Igniting the Fire Within," where we will delve into the art of unleashing your internal potential. Whether you are a student, a professional, or simply someone seeking personal growth, this chapter is designed to inspire and guide you towards becoming the best version of yourself.

It all begins with self-awareness. Understanding who you are, your strengths, weaknesses, and passions, is fundamental to unlocking your internal potential. Take the time to reflect on your journey so far, your accomplishments, and the obstacles you have overcome. Embrace the lessons learned and embrace the unique qualities that make you who you are.

Once you have gained a deeper understanding of yourself, it is time to set goals that align with your true aspirations. Identify what you want to achieve and create a roadmap to success. Remember, these goals should be challenging yet attainable, pushing you to grow and evolve. As you progress towards your objectives, make sure to celebrate your small victories along the way. This will fuel your motivation and keep the fire burning.

In addition to self-awareness and goal-setting, another essential aspect of unleashing your internal potential is cultivating a positive mindset. Believe in your capabilities and banish self-doubt. Surround yourself with supportive individuals who inspire and uplift you. Embrace challenges as opportunities for growth and learn from setbacks. By adopting a positive mindset, you will tap into your full potential and attract opportunities that align with your desires.

Furthermore, continuous learning is a key component of unleashing your internal potential. Stay curious, seek out new knowledge, and never stop growing. Explore different fields, read books, attend workshops, and engage in conversations with experts in your areas of interest. Remember, knowledge is power, and by expanding your horizons, you open up new doors of possibility.

In conclusion, "Igniting the Fire Within" is a subchapter dedicated to helping you unleash your internal potential. By focusing on self-awareness, goal-setting, cultivating a positive mindset, and continuous learning, you can tap into the fire that burns within you. Embrace the journey, believe in yourself, and become everything you can be. Your potential is limitless, and the world is waiting for you to shine.

Chapter 8: Unlocking Your Creativity and Imagination

Embracing the Power of Imagination

In our fast-paced and technology-driven world, it is easy to lose touch with our innate ability to imagine and create. However, it is through the power of imagination that we can truly tap into our internal potential and become everything we can be. In this subchapter, we will explore the importance of embracing the power of imagination and how it can transform our lives.

Imagination is not just for children; it is a powerful tool that can be harnessed by people of all ages. When we allow ourselves to imagine, we open up a world of possibilities. We can envision new solutions to problems, dream up innovative ideas, and even manifest our deepest desires. Imagination has the power to unlock our creative potential and propel us towards success in all aspects of our lives.

One of the reasons why imagination is so potent is that it allows us to envision a future that is different from our current reality. When we can see beyond the limitations of our circumstances, we are able to set ambitious goals and work towards achieving them. Imagination gives us the courage to step outside of our comfort zones and take risks, ultimately leading to personal growth and self-discovery.

Moreover, embracing the power of imagination helps us develop a positive mindset. By envisioning success and abundance, we attract positive energy and opportunities into our lives. Imagination fuels our belief in ourselves and our abilities, enabling us to overcome obstacles and persevere in the face of adversity. It empowers us to create the life we truly desire and deserve.

To tap into the power of imagination, it is essential to make space for creativity in our lives. This can be done through activities such as journaling, drawing, or engaging in hobbies that allow us to express ourselves freely. Taking time to daydream, meditate, or visualize our goals also helps to activate our imagination. By incorporating these practices into our daily routines, we can strengthen our ability to imagine and unleash our internal potential.

In conclusion, embracing the power of imagination is crucial for unleashing our internal potential and becoming everything we can be. By tapping into our creative minds, we can envision new possibilities, set ambitious goals, and manifest our dreams. Imagination empowers us to overcome challenges and develop a positive mindset, ultimately leading to personal growth and success. So, let us dare to imagine and unlock the limitless power within us.

Overcoming Creative Blocks

Subchapter: Overcoming Creative Blocks

Introduction:

In our pursuit of unleashing our internal potential, creativity plays a vital role. Whether you are an artist, writer, entrepreneur, or simply someone who wants to tap into their creative side, understanding and overcoming creative blocks is essential. In this subchapter, we will explore the various reasons behind creative blocks and provide practical strategies to overcome them. By harnessing the power of your imagination and overcoming these obstacles, you can truly be everything you can be.

Understanding Creative Blocks:

Creative blocks can manifest in different forms, hindering our ability to tap into our creative potential. Factors such as fear, self-doubt, lack of inspiration, and external pressures all contribute to creative blocks. Recognizing these barriers is the first step towards overcoming them.

Strategies to Overcome Creative Blocks:

1. Embrace vulnerability: Fear of failure often stifles our creativity. Accept that mistakes and setbacks are part of the creative process. Embrace vulnerability and allow yourself to take risks, as they often lead to breakthroughs.

2. Create a conducive environment: Surround yourself with inspiration. This can be in the form of books, art, music, or even nature. Designate a specific space for your creative endeavors, free from distractions, where you can fully immerse yourself in the process.

3. Practice mindfulness: Incorporate mindfulness techniques into your creative routine. Meditation and deep breathing exercises can help calm the mind, reduce anxiety, and enhance focus. By being present in the moment, you allow your creative energy to flow freely.

4. Seek diverse experiences: Engage in activities outside your comfort zone. Exploring new places, meeting different people, and trying unfamiliar things can spark fresh ideas and perspectives. Embrace the unknown and allow it to fuel your creativity.

5. Collaborate and share: Connect with like-minded individuals who share your passion for creativity. Collaboration can provide valuable feedback, encouragement, and fresh insights. Sharing your work with others not only helps you grow but also allows you to inspire and uplift others.

Conclusion:

In this subchapter, we have delved into the realm of creative blocks and explored effective strategies to overcome them. Remember, everyone encounters creative blocks at some point, but it is how we navigate through them that truly defines our potential. By embracing vulnerability, creating a conducive environment, practicing mindfulness, seeking diverse experiences, and collaborating with others, you can unleash your full creative potential. So, go forth and let your imagination soar, for within you lies the power to be everything you can be.

Thinking Outside the Box

In today's fast-paced world, where innovation and creativity are highly valued, the ability to think outside the box has become a crucial skill. Whether you are a student, a professional, or an entrepreneur, thinking outside the box can help you unlock your internal potential and achieve extraordinary success. In this subchapter, we will explore the power of thinking outside the box and how it can transform your life.

Thinking outside the box refers to the ability to approach problems and challenges with a fresh perspective and unconventional solutions. It is about breaking free from the limitations of traditional thinking and exploring new possibilities. When you think outside the box, you tap into your creative mind, allowing you to see opportunities where others see obstacles. It is a mindset that pushes you to question the status quo, challenge conventional wisdom, and discover innovative solutions.

As humans, we are creatures of habit, often relying on familiar patterns and established routines. However, by thinking outside the box, we break free from the confines of our comfort zones and open ourselves up to new ideas and experiences. This mindset shift enables us to embrace change, adapt to new situations, and seize opportunities that others may overlook.

Thinking outside the box requires us to cultivate a curious and open mind. It encourages us to explore diverse perspectives, seek out new knowledge, and engage in continuous learning. By expanding our horizons and exposing ourselves to different cultures, industries, and disciplines, we broaden our understanding and enhance our ability to think creatively.

In a world that is constantly evolving and demanding innovative solutions, thinking outside the box has become a valuable skill in all aspects of life. Whether you are looking to advance in your career, start your own business, or simply improve your problem-solving abilities, embracing this mindset will set you apart from the crowd.

So, how can you start thinking outside the box? Begin by challenging your assumptions and questioning the status quo. Look for inspiration from different sources, such as literature, art, or nature. Surround yourself with diverse individuals who can offer fresh perspectives and stimulate your creativity. Embrace failure as a valuable learning opportunity and don't be afraid to take risks.

In conclusion, thinking outside the box is a powerful tool for unleashing your internal potential. By adopting this mindset, you will unlock your creativity, discover new possibilities, and achieve extraordinary success. So, dare to think differently, be open to change, and embrace the unknown. Your journey to unleashing your full potential begins when you step outside the box!

Expressing Yourself Through Various Artistic Mediums

Art has been a powerful means of self-expression since the dawn of human civilization. From cave paintings to modern digital art, artistic mediums have evolved, but their purpose remains the same: to provide a channel for individuals to unleash their internal potential and communicate their deepest emotions. In this subchapter, we explore the various artistic mediums that allow you to express yourself and tap into your creative energy.

Painting and drawing are perhaps the most widely known artistic mediums. With a brush or pencil in hand, you can create vibrant landscapes, abstract masterpieces, or intricate portraits that reflect your inner world. The strokes and colors you choose convey emotions, thoughts, and experiences, allowing you to tell your story visually.

Sculpture, on the other hand, enables you to transform raw materials into three-dimensional forms. From clay to stone, wood to metal, sculpting allows you to mold and shape your ideas into tangible objects. The process of physically working with your hands can be both therapeutic and empowering, as you witness your thoughts taking form before your eyes.

For those who prefer words as their artistic medium, writing allows you to explore the depths of your imagination and share your unique perspective with the world. Through poetry, prose, or storytelling, you can create entire universes, evoke powerful emotions, and inspire others. The written word has the power to transcend time and connect people across cultures and generations.

If music is your passion, then composing, singing, or playing an instrument becomes your language of expression. Whether you choose to write your own songs, interpret existing melodies, or simply lose yourself in the rhythm, music has an unparalleled ability to touch the soul. It allows you to communicate emotions that words alone cannot convey, forging a deep connection with your audience.

Photography, film, and dance are other artistic mediums that capture moments, movements, and stories. Photography freezes time, showcasing the beauty of the world through your unique lens. Film combines visual and auditory elements to create immersive experiences that can transport viewers to different realities. Dance, on the other hand, uses the body as a medium to express emotions, narratives, and cultural traditions.

Whatever artistic medium resonates with you, the key lies in embracing it wholeheartedly. By engaging in the creative process, you tap into your internal potential, unlocking a vast source of inspiration that can transform your life. So, whether you choose to paint, write, dance, or create in any other way, let your artistic endeavors be a reflection of your true self and a celebration of the power within.

Chapter 9: Nurturing Physical Well-being

Prioritizing Exercise and Movement

In today's fast-paced and sedentary lifestyle, it's easy to neglect the importance of exercise and movement. However, if you truly want to unleash your internal potential and become everything you can be, prioritizing physical activity is essential. In this subchapter, we will explore the numerous benefits of exercise and movement, and provide you with practical tips to incorporate them into your daily routine.

Exercise is not only crucial for maintaining physical health but also has a profound impact on mental and emotional well-being. Regular physical activity helps reduce the risk of chronic diseases, improves cardiovascular health, strengthens bones and muscles, and boosts the immune system. Moreover, exercise releases endorphins, the feel-good hormones, which elevate mood and reduce stress, anxiety, and depression.

To prioritize exercise and movement, it's important to identify activities that you enjoy and can easily incorporate into your lifestyle. Whether it's jogging, dancing, swimming, or practicing yoga, finding an activity that brings you joy will make it easier to stick to a routine. Start small and gradually increase the intensity and duration of your workouts to avoid burnout or injuries.

Another effective way to prioritize exercise is by scheduling it into your daily routine. Treat it as an important appointment with yourself that cannot be canceled or rescheduled. By blocking out time specifically for physical activity, you are sending a message to your subconscious mind that your health and well-being are a priority.

Additionally, it's crucial to remember that movement doesn't always have to be structured exercise. Incorporating small changes in your daily habits can make a significant difference. Take the stairs instead of the elevator, walk or bike instead of driving short distances, or simply stretch and move your body during breaks at work.

Remember, consistency is key. Aim for at least 150 minutes of moderate-intensity aerobic activity or 75 minutes of vigorous-intensity aerobic activity per week, along with muscle-strengthening activities twice a week. However, it's important to listen to your body and adjust the intensity and frequency of your workouts as needed.

By prioritizing exercise and movement, you are investing in your overall well-being and unlocking your full potential. Embrace the power of physical activity to enhance your energy levels, improve mental clarity, boost self-confidence, and cultivate a positive mindset. Make a commitment to yourself today and start unleashing your internal potential through exercise and movement.

Fueling Your Body with Nutritious Foods

In order to unleash your internal potential and be everything you can be, it is essential to fuel your body with nutritious foods. The food we consume has a direct impact on our physical and mental well-being, making it imperative to make mindful choices when it comes to what we eat. This subchapter delves into the importance of nourishing your body with wholesome foods and provides valuable insights on how to make healthier dietary choices.

Nutrition is the foundation of a healthy lifestyle. It provides our bodies with the essential nutrients, vitamins, and minerals needed for optimal functioning. When we fuel our bodies with nutritious foods, we provide the necessary components for growth, repair, and overall well-being. A balanced diet consisting of fruits, vegetables, whole grains, lean proteins, and healthy fats can boost energy levels, enhance cognitive function, and strengthen the immune system.

In today's fast-paced world, it is easy to succumb to the temptation of convenience foods that are often laden with unhealthy fats, sugars, and artificial additives. However, by consciously choosing to prioritize nutritious foods, we can unlock our full potential. Incorporating nutrient-dense foods into our diets can lead to increased focus, improved mood, and a higher level of productivity.

One key aspect of fueling your body with nutritious foods is understanding portion control. It is important to be mindful of the amounts of food we consume, as overeating can lead to weight gain and other health issues. By practicing portion control and listening to our bodies' hunger and fullness cues, we can maintain a healthy weight and optimize our energy levels.

Additionally, being aware of the quality of the food we consume is crucial. Opt for organic, locally-sourced, and minimally processed foods whenever possible. These choices not only provide more nutrients, but they also support sustainable farming practices and reduce our carbon footprint.

In conclusion, fueling your body with nutritious foods is a fundamental step in unleashing your internal potential. By making conscious choices to prioritize whole, nutrient-dense foods, you can optimize your physical and mental well-being. Remember to practice portion control and opt for high-quality, minimally processed foods to support your journey towards unleashing your full potential. Start today and witness the transformative power of nourishing your body from within.

Getting Adequate Rest and Sleep

In our fast-paced modern world, we often find ourselves caught up in the hustle and bustle of everyday life. We are constantly striving to achieve more, be more, and do more. However, in our pursuit of success and personal growth, we often overlook a crucial aspect of unleashing our internal potential - getting adequate rest and sleep.

Rest and sleep are not just luxuries; they are essential for our overall well-being and our ability to reach our full potential. When we are well-rested, our minds are sharper, our bodies are rejuvenated, and our creativity is enhanced. It is during periods of rest that our brains consolidate memories, repair tissues, and recharge our energy levels.

To truly unleash our internal potential, we must prioritize rest and sleep as integral parts of our daily routine. Here are some strategies to help you achieve optimal rest and sleep:

1. Set a consistent sleep schedule: Try to go to bed and wake up at the same time every day, even on weekends. This helps regulate your body's internal clock, ensuring better quality sleep.

2. Create a bedtime routine: Establishing a pre-sleep ritual signals to your body that it's time to wind down. This could include activities like reading, taking a warm bath, or practicing relaxation techniques.

3. Create a sleep-friendly environment: Make sure your bedroom is dark, quiet, and at a comfortable temperature. Invest in a comfortable mattress and pillows that support your body's needs.

4. Limit screen time before bed: The blue light emitted by electronic devices can disrupt our sleep patterns. Avoid using screens at least an hour before bedtime to allow your brain to wind down.

5. Practice stress management techniques: High levels of stress can interfere with sleep. Incorporate stress-reducing activities such as meditation, deep breathing exercises, or journaling into your daily routine.

6. Avoid stimulants: Limit your consumption of caffeine, nicotine, and alcohol, as these can negatively impact your sleep quality.

Remember, getting adequate rest and sleep is not a sign of laziness or weakness. It is a vital component of your journey towards unleashing your full potential. By prioritizing rest and sleep, you will find yourself more energized, focused, and ready to tackle any challenges that come your way.

So, take the time to nurture your mind and body through quality rest and sleep. Embrace the power of rejuvenation and unlock your internal potential like never before.

Promoting Holistic Health Practices

In today's fast-paced and highly demanding world, it is crucial to prioritize our well-being and take proactive steps towards achieving a balanced and fulfilling life. Holistic health practices offer a comprehensive approach to self-care, focusing on the integration of mind, body, and spirit. In this subchapter, we will explore the significance of promoting holistic health practices and how they can help you unleash your internal potential.

Holistic health practices encompass various aspects of our lives, including physical fitness, mental clarity, emotional well-being, and spiritual growth. By nurturing each of these dimensions, we create a harmonious and interconnected system that supports our overall health and empowers us to reach our full potential.

Physical fitness is a fundamental pillar of holistic health. Regular exercise, a balanced diet, and sufficient rest are essential for maintaining optimal physical well-being. Engaging in physical activities not only improves our physical strength and stamina but also boosts our mental clarity and emotional resilience.

Mental clarity and emotional well-being are equally vital components of holistic health. Practices such as meditation, mindfulness, and positive affirmations help us cultivate a calm and focused mind, enabling us to navigate challenges with clarity and resilience. By acknowledging and processing our emotions in a healthy manner, we can free ourselves from negativity and create space for personal growth.

Spiritual growth is another integral aspect of holistic health. It involves connecting with our inner selves, exploring our values, and finding a sense of purpose and meaning in life. Whether through religious practices, nature connection, or self-reflection, nurturing our spiritual well-being enhances our overall happiness and fulfillment.

Promoting holistic health practices can have transformative effects on our lives. By adopting these practices, we not only improve our physical health and mental well-being but also enhance our ability to pursue our passions and achieve our goals. The integration of mind, body, and spirit enables us to tap into our true potential and live a purposeful life.

In conclusion, embracing holistic health practices is essential for anyone seeking to unleash their internal potential. By prioritizing physical fitness, mental clarity, emotional well-being, and spiritual growth, we create a foundation for personal growth, happiness, and fulfillment. The power to unlock our full potential lies within us, and by promoting holistic health practices, we can harness that power and embark on a journey of self-discovery and self-actualization. Let this subchapter serve as a guide to inspire you to take the necessary steps towards promoting holistic health practices and unleashing your true potential.

Chapter 10: Taking Inspired Action

Setting Realistic and Actionable Goals

In order to fully unleash your internal potential and become everything you can be, it is essential to set realistic and actionable goals. Goals serve as a roadmap, guiding you towards the realization of your dreams. They provide focus, motivation, and a sense of direction in your journey to unlock your full potential. However, setting effective goals requires careful consideration and strategic planning.

Firstly, it is important to set realistic goals that align with your capabilities and circumstances. While it is admirable to dream big, setting unattainable goals may lead to disappointment and demotivation. By setting realistic goals, you can maintain a sense of achievement and constantly build upon your successes. Analyze your strengths, weaknesses, and available resources to determine what is within your grasp. Remember, small steps forward are still progress.

Additionally, actionable goals are vital for success. Rather than vague aspirations, actionable goals are specific, measurable, attainable, relevant, and time-bound (SMART). Clearly define what you want to achieve, break it down into smaller milestones, and assign deadlines. This way, you can track your progress and make necessary adjustments along the way. Take into account any potential obstacles or challenges that may arise and develop contingency plans to ensure you stay on track.

Moreover, it is crucial to align your goals with your passions and values. When your goals resonate with your deepest desires and core beliefs, you will find greater fulfillment and motivation in pursuing them. Reflect on what truly matters to you and how your goals contribute to your overall vision of a fulfilling life. This alignment will fuel your determination and enthusiasm, propelling you forward even in the face of adversity.

Lastly, remember that goal setting is an ongoing process. As you progress and evolve, your goals may need to be adjusted or refined. Be open to reevaluating your objectives and adapting them to new circumstances or insights. Embrace the lessons learned from each experience and use them to inform your future goals. This flexibility and willingness to learn will contribute to your growth and the unlocking of your full potential.

In conclusion, setting realistic and actionable goals is a crucial step in unleashing your internal potential. By being mindful of your capabilities, setting SMART goals, aligning with your passions, and remaining adaptable, you will embark on a journey towards personal growth and fulfillment. Remember, the power to achieve greatness lies within you – take the first step and set your goals today.

Implementing Effective Strategies for Progress

In the pursuit of personal growth and unleashing our full potential, it is essential to have a clear roadmap and effective strategies in place. This subchapter focuses on implementing these strategies to ensure progress and success on our journey towards becoming everything we can be.

1. Setting Clear Goals: The first step towards progress is defining specific and measurable goals. By setting clear objectives, we can create a sense of direction and purpose. These goals act as beacons, guiding us towards our desired outcomes and motivating us to take action.

2. Developing Action Plans: Once we have established our goals, it is crucial to develop well-defined action plans. These plans outline the necessary steps and milestones required to achieve our objectives. Breaking down our goals into smaller, manageable tasks makes them more attainable and allows us to track our progress effectively.

3. Cultivating Discipline and Consistency: Progress requires discipline and consistency. It is essential to develop and maintain habits that support our goals. By committing to consistent action, we build

momentum and create a positive feedback loop that fuels our progress. Embracing a growth mindset helps us overcome obstacles and stay focused on our journey.

4. Embracing Continuous Learning: Progress is not a destination but a lifelong journey. To keep moving forward, we must embrace continuous learning. Seeking new knowledge, acquiring new skills, and staying up-to-date with the latest trends in our field empowers us to adapt and grow. Learning from both successes and failures allows us to refine our strategies and improve our chances of success.

5. Building a Supportive Network: Surrounding ourselves with like-minded individuals who support our goals is crucial for progress. A strong support network provides encouragement, guidance, and accountability. By connecting with mentors, coaches, and peers who share our aspirations, we can gain valuable insights and access resources that accelerate our progress.

6. Tracking and Celebrating Milestones: Regularly tracking our progress is essential for staying on course and making necessary adjustments. Celebrating milestones along the way reinforces our motivation and provides a sense of accomplishment. Acknowledging our achievements boosts our confidence and fuels further progress.

In conclusion, implementing effective strategies for progress is vital in our journey to unleash our internal potential. By setting clear goals, developing action plans, cultivating discipline, embracing continuous learning, building a supportive network, and tracking our progress, we ensure steady growth and success. Remember, progress may be challenging at times, but with determination and the right strategies, we can overcome any obstacles and unlock our full potential.

Persevering Through Challenges

In the journey of unleashing our full potential, we often encounter numerous challenges that test our resilience, determination, and inner strength. These obstacles can arise in various aspects of our lives, including career, relationships, health, and personal growth. However, it is through persevering through these challenges that we truly tap into the power within us and unlock our internal potential.

Challenges are an inevitable part of life, and it is how we respond to them that defines our character and shapes our future. Instead of viewing challenges as roadblocks, we must embrace them as opportunities for growth and self-discovery. It is during these trying times that we unearth our hidden strengths and develop the necessary skills to overcome adversity.

Perseverance is the key to navigating through challenges. It requires a steadfast commitment to our goals and an unwavering belief in our abilities. When faced with setbacks or failures, we must cultivate a resilient mindset that allows us to bounce back stronger than before. Each challenge we overcome adds to our arsenal of experiences, making us more equipped to handle future obstacles.

One of the most crucial aspects of persevering through challenges is maintaining a positive mindset. It is easy to be consumed by negativity and self-doubt when faced with daunting hurdles. However, by shifting our focus to the lessons and opportunities that lie within these challenges, we can reframe our thinking and find the motivation to move forward. Surrounding ourselves with a supportive network of individuals who believe in our potential also plays a pivotal role in keeping our spirits high during tough times.

Moreover, perseverance requires patience and flexibility. It is essential to understand that progress may not always be linear, and setbacks are part of the journey. Embracing a growth mindset allows us to adapt to new circumstances and find alternative paths towards our goals. It is through these detours that we often discover new strengths and opportunities we may have never considered before.

In conclusion, persevering through challenges is a fundamental aspect of unleashing our internal potential. By embracing obstacles as opportunities for growth, maintaining a positive mindset, and cultivating resilience, we can overcome any hurdles that come our way. Our ability to persevere not only shapes our character but also propels us towards reaching our true potential. So, let us face challenges head-on, knowing that within them lies the power to transform ourselves and become everything we can be.

Celebrating Personal Growth and Milestones

Subchapter: Celebrating Personal Growth and Milestones

Introduction:

In our journey to unleash our full potential, celebrating personal growth and milestones is an essential aspect that often goes overlooked. As we strive to be everything we can be and tap into our internal potential, it is crucial to acknowledge and appreciate the progress we make along the way. This subchapter will explore the significance of celebrating personal growth and milestones, providing valuable insights and practical strategies for the readers.

Recognizing the Power of Personal Growth:

Personal growth is a powerful force that drives us towards achieving our goals and realizing our dreams. It involves continuous learning, self-reflection, and stepping out of our comfort zones. By acknowledging and celebrating our personal growth, we not only boost our self-confidence but also reinforce our motivation to keep pushing forward.

Importance of Milestones:

Milestones are markers of progress that indicate how far we have come along our journey. They can be big or small, tangible or intangible, but each milestone deserves recognition. Celebrating milestones allows us to appreciate our accomplishments, providing a sense of fulfillment and encouragement to keep striving for greatness.

The Power of Celebration:

Celebration is a powerful tool that amplifies positive emotions, strengthens bonds, and boosts overall well-being. It allows us to savor the joy of personal growth and milestones, reminding us of our capabilities and potential. By celebrating our achievements, we create a positive feedback loop that fuels further growth and propels us towards even greater success.

Practical Strategies for Celebrating Personal Growth and Milestones:

1. Reflect and Acknowledge: Take time to reflect on your journey, acknowledge the progress you have made, and appreciate the lessons learned along the way.

2. Set Milestones and Goals: Break down your larger goals into smaller achievable milestones. Celebrate each milestone as you reach them, providing motivation to keep moving forward.

3. Create Rituals: Develop personal rituals or traditions to commemorate your achievements. This could involve treating yourself to something special, sharing your success with loved ones, or even journaling about your progress.

4. Share and Inspire: Celebrate your growth and milestones with others, sharing your journey to inspire and motivate those around you. By

celebrating together, you create a supportive community that encourages personal growth for everyone involved.

Conclusion:

Celebrating personal growth and milestones is an integral part of unleashing our full potential. It not only boosts our self-confidence and motivation but also reinforces the positive feedback loop that propels us towards even greater success. By taking the time to reflect, set milestones, create rituals, and share with others, we embrace the power within us and inspire those around us to do the same. So let us celebrate our growth, honor our milestones, and continue on our journey to becoming everything we can be.

Conclusion: Embracing Your Full Potential

Reflecting on Your Journey

In life, we often find ourselves caught up in the hustle and bustle of daily routines, chasing after success and external validation. We forget to pause and reflect on our own journey, to truly understand who we are and the limitless potential that lies within us. In this subchapter, titled "Reflecting on Your Journey," we will delve deep into the importance of self-reflection and how it can help us unleash our internal potential.

Self-reflection is a powerful tool that allows us to gain clarity, self-awareness, and a deeper understanding of our own strengths and weaknesses. It offers us a chance to evaluate our past experiences, the lessons we have learned, and the progress we have made. By taking the time to reflect on our journey, we can identify patterns, recognize our growth, and acknowledge the areas where we need to improve.

One of the key benefits of self-reflection is gaining a heightened sense of self-awareness. It enables us to become more conscious of our thoughts, emotions, and behaviors, thus helping us make better decisions and take actions aligned with our true selves. By reflecting on our journey, we can uncover our passions, values, and purpose, allowing us to shape our lives in a way that aligns with our authentic selves.

Furthermore, self-reflection provides an opportunity for personal growth and development. By analyzing our past experiences, we can identify the obstacles we have overcome, the skills we have acquired, and the areas where we have excelled. This self-awareness can serve as a catalyst for setting new goals, pushing our boundaries, and unleashing our full potential.

Throughout this subchapter, we will explore various techniques and exercises that can facilitate self-reflection. From journaling and meditation to seeking feedback from trusted individuals, each tool will empower you to pause, introspect, and gain valuable insights about your journey.

Remember, unleashing your internal potential requires a deep understanding of yourself. It necessitates acknowledging your strengths, embracing your weaknesses, and harnessing your unique qualities. By reflecting on your journey, you will discover the power within you to be everything you can be.

So, take a moment to pause, to reflect, and to embark on a journey of self-discovery. Unleash your internal potential and embrace the incredible person you are capable of becoming. This subchapter will guide you on this transformative path, providing the tools and insights needed to reflect on your journey and unlock the power within.

Embracing the Power Within

In our modern society, we often find ourselves consumed by external factors that shape our lives. We are bombarded with expectations, social norms, and the constant pursuit of success. However, amidst this chaos, we often forget the most essential aspect of our being - the power within us. It is this power that holds the key to unlocking our full potential and living a fulfilled life. Welcome to the subchapter titled "Embracing the Power Within" from the book "The Power Within: A Journey to Unleashing Your Full Potential."

To truly be everything you can be, it is crucial to tap into your internal potential. This subchapter explores the concept of embracing the power within and delves into the various ways you can unleash your internal potential. It serves as a guide for individuals from all walks of life, as everyone possesses untapped power within themselves waiting to be discovered.

The power within is not something new or foreign, but rather an inherent part of our existence. It is the voice that urges us to dream big, to believe in ourselves, and to trust our instincts. By acknowledging and embracing this power, we can overcome self-doubt and fear, and embark on a transformative journey towards self-actualization.

Throughout this subchapter, you will discover practical strategies and exercises to connect with your inner power. From meditation and mindfulness techniques to self-reflection and goal setting, each step will bring you closer to unleashing the dormant potential within.

Moreover, this subchapter emphasizes the importance of self-care and self-love. By nurturing our minds, bodies, and souls, we create a strong foundation for our internal power to flourish. It offers insights into developing healthy habits, maintaining a positive mindset, and embracing self-compassion.

Whether you are a young professional seeking career growth, a student navigating the path to self-discovery, or a parent striving to be the best version of yourself, this subchapter is for you. It is a call to action, encouraging you to step out of your comfort zone, embrace your unique strengths, and live a purposeful life.

So, embark on this transformative journey of self-discovery and unlock the power within you. By embracing your internal potential, you will not only enhance your own life but also inspire those around you. The world is waiting for the full expression of your unique gifts and talents. It's time to embrace the power within and become everything you can be.

Continuing the Path of Personal Growth and Fulfillment

In this subchapter, we will dive deeper into the journey of personal growth and fulfillment, exploring how you can continue to unleash your internal potential and be everything you can be. It is a quest that transcends all boundaries and is relevant to every individual, regardless of age, background, or aspirations.

As humans, we have an inherent desire to grow and evolve. It is through personal growth that we discover our true potential and unlock the power within us. However, the path to personal growth is not a destination but a continuous journey. It requires commitment, resilience, and a willingness to embrace change.

One of the key aspects of continuing this path is self-awareness. Understanding ourselves, our strengths, weaknesses, and values is crucial in determining the direction we want to take. Reflecting on our experiences, seeking feedback, and constantly learning about ourselves allows us to make informed choices and strive for personal growth.

Another important element is setting goals. By defining clear and achievable objectives, we create a roadmap for our personal growth. These goals should be aligned with our values and aspirations, and they should challenge us to step out of our comfort zones. Regularly reviewing and readjusting our goals ensures that we stay on track and continue to grow.

Embracing a growth mindset is also essential. Believing that our abilities and intelligence can be developed through dedication and hard work empowers us to take on challenges and learn from failures. Embracing a growth mindset enables us to see setbacks as opportunities for growth and fuels our motivation to keep moving forward.

Additionally, surrounding ourselves with a supportive network is crucial. Connecting with like-minded individuals who share our passion for personal growth and fulfillment creates an environment that fosters growth. Engaging in meaningful conversations, seeking mentorship, and collaborating with others allows us to gain new perspectives and learn from the experiences of those who have walked a similar path.

Lastly, self-care and well-being play a significant role in sustaining personal growth. Nurturing our physical, mental, and emotional health ensures that we have the energy and resilience to continue on this journey. Practices such as mindfulness, exercise, and self-reflection help us maintain a healthy balance in our lives and stay connected to our inner selves.

Continuing the path of personal growth and fulfillment requires dedication, self-awareness, and a commitment to lifelong learning. By embracing these principles and taking intentional steps towards our goals, we can unleash our internal potential and become everything we can be. Remember, the journey never ends; it is a continual process of self-discovery and growth that leads to a life of fulfillment and purpose.